LIVE BOLDLY

WORKBOOK

EPISODES 31-45

BY: NICKI CORINNE WHITE

LIVE
BOLDLY

*LIVING INTENTIONALLY
IN TODAY'S WORLD*

WORKBOOK

EPISODES 31-45

Published by Carpenter's Son Publishing, Franklin, TN

Front cover artwork by Nicki Corinne White
design by Debbie Manning Sheppard
ISBN: 978-1-956370-57-7
Printed in the United States of America

DEDICATION

TO ALL MY BIBLE STUDY PARTNERS

I am thinking about all the many, many Bible studies I have been to over the past 35 years or so. The women who poured Scripture into me. Who laughed and cried with me. Who prayed for me and with me, for years. Being able to meet regularly with others does many things. It holds you steady when you don't really want to study. You may not even want to meet with anyone, but you go anyway. Guess what? You always end up being thankful you went. God uses other people in our life to stir us up for love and good deeds. When I have been down spiritually, it has been my Bible study partners who have encouraged me, prayed for me, and even scolded me a bit. They held me accountable to who they knew I loved. God. I am so very grateful for these people in my life.

About eight years ago or so, I began teaching New Inductive Study Series Precepts classes that are a Bible study series for each book of the Bible. Some studies have more than one book of the Bible in them. They are 13 week courses, so we do at least 2 books per year. We have now completed studying over 40 of the 66 books of the Bible! Many different people have been involved, and our classes usually average 2-6 people. In the past 5 years, Amy Crist has been faithful in coming each year. I am sharing this with you because I have so enjoyed meeting with this young woman for the past few years, and sharing our hearts. We have prayed, studied and shed tears for loved ones.

These Live Boldly workbooks are a tool our team has created for you to study and use to share your heart with others. That is what mentoring and discipleship is all about. It encourages us to grow, helps us through trials, and rejoices in our joys.

I am praying for you, dear one. That you grow in the grace of our Lord, so that you too can share with others.

LIVE BOLDLY MINISTRIES TEAM

- CRAIG WHITE - husband, tech support, video editor, graphics
- JESSICA EVERETT - daughter, executive administrator, scheduling, emails, social media, marketing, basically everything
- MAUREEN LOEFFLER - editor, tech support, advisor
- MARSHA PHILBROOK - editor
- JAMIE HUDSON - photographer
- RUTHANNE BEDDOE - spiritual advisor, prayer team
- LISA SHUMAKER - sister, Col 3:12 Ministries research team, marketing
- AMY CRIST - special projects
- ASHLEY TAYLOR - Col 3:12 Ministries research team
- KAREN LAW - Col 3:12 Ministries research team, libraries
- RAFAEL AMARO - tech, website
- LINDA SARACOFF - photographer, social media
- GABRIELLE BOLIOU - special projects, prayer team
- JEANETTE DICKEY - prayer team, libraries
- NANCY JINDRICH - prayer team
- DEBBIE MERRITT - prayer team
- COURTNEY JORDAN - prayer team
- CINDY SMITH - prayer team
- PRISCILLA ROBINSON - prayer team
- JIM AND KAREN HERD - prayer team, social media
- JONI SULLIVAN BAKER, Buoyancy PR - She has encouraged me, been patient with me as a new author and been easy to approach with my many questions.
- Also my editor, TAMMY KLING, who gave me the great idea to do a video series and these workbooks. She is a worldchanger!

TABLE OF CONTENTS

INTRODUCTION

In 2020, when Covid hit, we all "thought" that things would open up in just a couple months, and life would go back to normal. Ha! Then we "thought" that maybe by Fall things would normalize. Ha! It really took us by surprise. I wrote my book ***"BOLD: Living Intentionally In Today's World"*** because God is still on the throne, and we still need to serve even when life suddenly takes an unexpected turn. My editor called me that fall and encouraged me to do a weekly video series, and then eventually do workbooks to go with the series. For 45 weeks I sat in front of a ring light in my workroom and did 15 minute videos. They encouraged people to share the gospel, and to get out of their comfort zone and help others. I broke the video series up into three 15 episode workbooks.

This is the third workbook. It covers episodes 31- 45. It begins by sharing about Godly men and women who lived radically for God. The final few chapters encourage us to not grow weary in doing good, and serving Him with all our heart.

Each episode can be watched either on our Facebook group Live Boldly or on our YouTube channel under Nicki Corinne White. We hope you enjoy!

Find all the videos for this workbook on
YouTube@nickicorinnewhite7299
(episodes 31-45)

EPISODE 31

RADICALS

I am sure you have all admired a believer who gave everything for God. I have studied several who have been thought of as "radicals". Two people who were radical for God were somewhat linked, although they lived thousands of miles apart: Hudson Taylor and Amy Carmichael. Amy had heard of what Hudson had done in China, was inspired by his faith, and decided God was calling her also into foreign missions.

Both came from homes with devoted Christian parents. Both dressed like the people in the country where they were serving. And both wanted to live life like those whom they served. They both served their entire lives, as with God there is no retirement age.

QUESTIONS

1. **Hudson Taylor spent a lot of time in preparation before he left England. He studied the Mandarin language. When he finally went to China, he took Bibles and tracts to give out. After a few years he switched from serving with one missionary agency and he formed the China Inland Mission. He prayed for 24 missionaries to go to all the provinces of China, and God provided the people. These missionaries had no guaranteed income and had to provide for themselves. They dressed and ate like the Chinese people they were there to help. A truly radical idea at the time! In 1886 he prayed for 100 missionaries to go to China, and 102 went. He wrote, "China is not to be won by quiet, ease-loving men and women, the stamp of men and women we need is such as will put Jesus, (China) and souls first and foremost in everything and at every time, --and even life itself must be secondary." This is the life of someone who decided he would sacrifice all for the gospel. Not all of us have the ability to do this even if we firmly believe in it.**

   Read Romans 2:1-2 & 9-21, and Mark 12:33. What are ways we CAN sacrifice?

   ____

   ____

   ____

   ____

2. **Hudson Taylor's life and faith were an inspiration to many. He had many health problems that at times kept him from living in China. He said, "I am so weak that I cannot read my bible, even pray. I can only lie still in God's arms like a little child and trust." There is so much we can do even if we don't feel great. We can trust God. We can pray for God to provide others to do the work we can't. Hudson prayed for more people to go to China to share the good news of Jesus.**

   What and who can you pray for today?

   ____

____

____

____

3. *Now let us look at Amy Carmichael. She served her community with her family for many years and worked in the slum areas of Belfast and Manchester. She went to a convention and heard Hudson Taylor speak about China Inland Mission. She decided to become a missionary. When in India, she felt burdened to rescue girls who were slaves and temple prostitutes at the Hindu temples. She founded the Dohnavur Fellowship in 1901 and later also helped young boys in need. Amy remained in India for 55 years without returning to her native Ireland. Her agency continues on today all these years later.*

   She wrote many books. I was given her book, "If" when I was in college. I was going through a struggle and each page was a comfort to me. Two other books she wrote are "God's Missionaries" and "Edges of His Ways". A couple of my favorite quotes from her that show her devotion to Christ are: "If I covet any place on earth but the dust at the foot of the cross, then I know nothing of Calvary's love." and "How can we follow the Savior far, who have no wound or scar?".

   Can you imagine 55 years and no break, no vacation, no trips to see her family? My husband and I are involved in a number of ministry activities during the week. We have a group Bible study in our home on Tuesdays, and help in the AWANA kids Bible program at our church on Wednesdays. I teach a ladies Precepts Bible study class on Thursdays, and every other week I am involved in a neighborhood Bible study. I will confess that sometimes I feel exhausted even though I love these ministries. But it is not the same sacrifice that missionaries do every day for years. I am not saying it is for everyone. I would pray that we all seek how God wants us to minister to those around us. Pray right now and ask how you can serve or better serve in the ministry you are involved with currently.

   Look up Matthew 25:35-40, 1 Peter 4:10-11, and Ephesians 6:7-8. What are ways we can serve others where we are?

____

____

4. ***Is there a ministry that you have yearned to help with? When I was a new believer as a teen, we had missionaries home on furlough who were visiting our church during their break from their ministry in Brazil. They had 3 teen boys, and I was sure I was meant to go to the mission field. Haha. This is not really what I am referring to, however, I must admit that meeting them did fuel my heart for serving. 40+ years later I still think of that time and through the years we have been involved with many missionaries' ministries. Can you think of missionaries you admire? Are you familiar with their needs? Do you write to them, send packages or host families when they come home? Many will tell you how valuable it is even to get an email.***

   Read 1 Peter 4:10-11, Matthew 5:16, 1 Samuel 12:24, Galatians 5:13, Hebrews 6:10. How do these verses inspire you to serve? What will you do this week to encourage and serve someone who is sacrificing for God?

5. ***Maybe you don't know any people who have gone to another country to share the good news of salvation through Jesus. Do you know of anyone who shares the gospel in large or small ways in your area? Someone who inspires you to be bold in your faith?***

   List three steps you can follow to share your faith with others.

EPISODE 32

DANIEL'S AMAZING FAITHFULNESS

Daniel is one of the first people in the Bible who comes to mind when I think of faithfulness to God. He was completely obedient to God. I got to thinking how little kids learn about Daniel in the lions' den and God shutting the lions' mouths, but as adults we need to see the bigger picture: Daniel's faithfulness and God's faithfulness. I think one of my favorite verses in the book of Daniel is 6:16, where King Darius says to Daniel,

> *"Your God whom you constantly serve will Himself deliver you".*

The King knew of Daniel's faith in God. Daniel's life was an example of steadfastness and consistency in his faith to everyone, even the king! This is an encouragement to all of us as we live out our faith.

We too are being watched constantly. Will others see that the mighty God we serve is powerful? Let's take a closer look.

QUESTIONS

1. The book of Daniel is to the Old Testament what Revelation is to the New Testament: it is full of prophecy. It covers the entire time period of the Babylonian captivity. Nine of the twelve chapters relate to prophecies given in dreams.

   The book begins in 605 BC when Babylon attacked Jerusalem. Daniel was taken away to Babylon with his three friends and many others. Other prophets had forewarned Israel what would happen as a result of their unbelief and disobedience. God allowed Israel to suffer because of their disobedience, but He loved them and would bring them back to Himself. Then they would see God's power when He would send the Messiah. The book of Daniel was written to encourage those exiled Jews. It begins by telling how Daniel and his three friends stand up for what they know God wanted them to do.

   Read Daniel 1:8-9. How does Daniel's obedience encourage you to be steadfast?

   ____

   ____

   ____

2. Read Daniel 1:10-20. Daniel and his friends were trained to be leaders in Babylon. Their names were changed, and they were told to eat a specific diet which included meat that had been sacrificed to idols. They refused and ate a healthy diet. The king found them 10 times healthier, better than the other men. The king respected them for their resolve. Following God's ways made Daniel and his friends stand out from the other young men, and the end result could have been disastrous, but God honored their faith. This is a great example to us as we work and are friends with others who may not be believers.

   Read the following verses. What do these verses tell us about steadfastness?

   James 1:12 ____

   ____

____

I Corinthians 15:58 ______________________________

____

____

____

2 Peter 3:17-18 ______________________________

____

____

____

Matthew 25:21 ______________________________

____

____

____

3. ***Later, the king made a golden image for the people to bow down and worship. Daniel's friends refused. The three friends were thrown into a blazing furnace but were not injured. God protected them. Years later, the other leaders of the land were not happy with Daniel because he was faithful, worked hard and was not corrupt, and the king was going to make Daniel head over all the other leaders. They convinced the king to make a decree that anyone who prayed to anyone or anything other than the king during a 30 day period would be thrown in the lions' den. This was done to trap Daniel, as he was known to pray regularly to God. When those leaders told the king that Daniel disobeyed the king's decree, the king was distressed but could not do anything to keep Daniel from being put into the lions' den. Because the king had seen Daniel's faithfulness to God for years, he knew Daniel's God would rescue him.***

   Read chapters 3 and 6 of Daniel. Like Daniel, our lives are watched by others. People notice when we stand up for what is right, for the truth, and for the things in our life that God wants us to do.

Who is watching you?

Write down the names of family members, friends, co-workers, etc. who might be impacted by your actions and attitudes.

____

____

____

____

____

4. ***The word "steadfastness" means "firmness in purpose, resolution, faith". List 5 ways you can exhibit your steadfastness and faithfulness to God even in the face of persecution, ridicule or indifference.***

____

____

____

____

____

EPISODE 33

THE UNASSUMING MIGHTY INFLUENTIAL MEN

I have been studying the lives of Jesus' disciples more this past year. We have discussed them a bit in the past, and I have to admit, I can relate to these men in many ways. I am sure you do too. They were called and followed, but most likely had no clue what they were being called to do. These men changed the world after Jesus' death, resurrection and ascension. They were the leaders of the early church as it was persecuted and spread far and wide. They would become the leaders of a movement like the world had never seen. Their influence would last forever.

QUESTIONS

1. **The word "disciple" means "student" in Greek. We've discussed discipleship and mentoring and the importance of it in our lives before. One of the aspects of discipleship is spending time with someone; sharing life. The disciples were with Jesus every day for three years. They needed to be so they could hear and learn all He wanted to share with them. And in turn others would learn from THEM. They learned so they could teach others. That is what discipleship is all about. Christ used these men, even though they did not have an extreme amount of spiritual understanding at first. They had to be reminded of truths over and over. Jesus mentored them as he was with them, day in and day out. Mentoring is crazy important.**

   Did you have a godly person who taught you and poured themselves into your life? Who has done that and how have they encouraged you?

   ____

   ____

   ____

   ____

2. **The second chapter of Acts describes the beginning of the church. This section is so important to me. It always convicts me to spend time with others.**

   Read about the ingathering of believers in Acts 2:36-47. What does it say the believers were doing together?

   ____

   ____

   ____

   ____

   ____

God can use you to encourage others. As we spend time and grow together, others can see what we have in Jesus and want it too.

3. ***The disciples were ordinary men but they listened and learned while spending time with Jesus. They were chosen by Jesus and they were used by God. We too can be used in big ways no matter who we are. Here are a few passages on mentoring: Titus 2:4-5; 1 Peter 5:2-3; 1 Corinthians 11:1; Romans 15:14; Hebrews 10:24-25; Philippians 3:17.***

   Which verse(s) encourages you the most to mentor someone? Did you learn something new about discipleship? What?

   ____

   ____

   ____

   ____

   ____

   ____

4. ***Do you have people in your life that you have wanted to spend time with and encourage? Don't delay. Pray for motivation to follow through. I know that I may be reminded of someone and then totally forget about it. I have to write it down.***

   Write down who you want to connect with soon.

   ____

   ____

   ____

   ____

   ____

EPISODE 34

TRUMPETS AND SPIES

I love the book of Joshua. The Israelites cross over the river into the long awaited promised land. The name "Joshua" means "Jehovah saves", or the "Lord is salvation". Joshua was commissioned by Moses, and was filled with the spirit of wisdom as stated in Deuteronomy 34:9:

> *"Now Joshua the son of Nun was filled with the spirit of wisdom, for Moses had laid his hands on him; and the sons of Israel listened to him and did as the Lord had commanded."*

Joshua was born into slavery in Egypt and was trained by Moses. The book of Joshua tells of the fulfillment of the promise of giving the land to Abraham's descendants. Joshua was a selfless man, following what God wanted him to do.

Hopefully this lesson will show you that you too can act on your faith to follow what God has for you to do.

QUESTIONS

1. **After Moses died, God spoke to Joshua telling him what he must do to cross the Jordan, and that He would give the land to the Israelites as promised. God told him that no man would be able to stand before him, and that He would not fail Joshua.**

   Read Joshua 1:9. Have you had a time in your life where you felt you could not move forward? How did God give you direction?

   ____

   ____

   ____

   ____

   ____

2. **Before Joshua could take the Israelites across the Jordan River into the land that was promised to them, a lot had to take place. He sent out spies to scout the land and the city of Jericho. They needed valuable information to assist the tribes of Israel before they could invade. These men needed to know about food, topography, and other things about the area. They needed a place where they could observe the town, and from where they could make a quick getaway.**

   Read Joshua 2:1-14.The spies were not there to take advantage of Rahab, but to use her house to plan a strategy. What did Rahab do for the spies?

   ____

   ____

   ____

   ____

   ____

3. ***They came to the house of Rahab, a prostitute and a product of a corrupt culture, whose home was near the gate. She was an immoral woman but this story is not about how hopeless she was. It is about God's redemption and love for her. No matter who she was, God would still save her and use her. Rahab had heard about the Israelites crossing the Red Sea and knew God would help them again. She believed enough to risk her life.***

   Read Hebrews 11:31. God wanted the spies to show Rahab grace. She is a great example of saving faith. She was at the bottom of the social ladder, BUT she would end up being a part of the Messianic line of Jesus, one of his ancestors! This is a great encouragement to me that no matter what our past, what mistakes we have made, and no matter what our present circumstances, God is mighty to save and has a great plan for our life.

   How does the story of this woman encourage you?

   ____

   ____

   ____

   ____

   ____

4. ***None of us is without sin. Rahab tells a lie in Joshua 2:3-6. God commends her faith, not the lying. Not only does Rahab save the lives of the two spies but her entire family as well. Finish reading the rest of the chapter (Joshua 2:15-24).***

   Even though we sin, God can use us no matter what. Rahab trusted that God was powerful enough to take care of her, and powerful enough to save her whole family. She had confidence in God.

   Do you trust that God is powerful enough to take care of that insurmountable issue, that problem that seems to have no solution, that impending disaster? What can you believe God for "by faith"?

   ____

   ____

5. *Now read James 2:24-26. We too can act on faith. We are more than conquerors. We can be examples to others around us.*

List 3 ways you can faithfully pray God will use your life for His purposes.

EPISODE 35

THE DRIVING FORCE

My first two books dealt more with overcoming adversity, helping others, and using your faith to encourage others. When I would sign a book I would always add Colossians 3:12 under my name. Then, when "BOLD: Living Intentionally In Today's World" came out, I decided I needed to use a different verse to add under my signature. After working in AWANA children's ministry for 30 years, the first thing that popped into my head was Romans 1:16,

> *"For I am not ashamed of the gospel for it is the power of God to salvation for everyone who believes, to the Jew first and also to the Greek."*

You see, we need to feel that sense of urgency to share our faith with everyone we know. I too can feel my heart pound with some nervousness when sharing sometimes, but I have to admit, the more I do it the easier it becomes. BUT, the bottom line...we absolutely cannot be ashamed of being a believer. So how do we get to that point?

QUESTIONS

1. **Read 1 Peter 3. This chapter stresses that we should always be willing to share our faith with meekness and reverence. We should be peacemakers, but speak the truth.**

   Read Proverbs 28:1 and 2 Timothy 1:7.

   What are ways that you feel comfortable sharing with someone? What holds you back? Why?

   ____

   ____

   ____

   ____

   ____

2. ***I too have that heart pounding moment where I stop and feel inadequate, unprepared, or unworthy. But when God gives us an opportunity to share with others, He will give us the courage.* Read the following verses. How will God help us?**

   Matthew 17:20 ______________________________________

   ____

   ____

   Luke 12:12: ____

   ____

   ____

3. **What happens when we do share our faith with others?**

   Ephesians 4:15-16: ___________________________________

   ____

James 2:17-26 ______________________________

4. **Here are some ways to prepare you for sharing your faith.**

    Practice sharing your testimony.

    Pray for opportunity.

    Role play.

    Memorize verses that you could share.

    Write out the verses you have memorized or want to memorize.

5. ***I love the Sermon on the Mount. In Matthew 5:6 Jesus says,***

    "Blessed are those who hunger and thirst for righteousness..."

    What does this mean? It is like an active spiritual longing. We should crave time with Him, long to spend time with Him. It also means that you long to live a godly life.

    I have so many favorite Psalms, but I admit to loving those where David cries out to God. Sometimes he is upset, BUT he always ends the Psalm by praising God. David was a man after God's own heart. He was so very honest and communicated with God without holding anything back. David complained,

told God his troubles, and even cried. He spent time with God. Knowing God, His mercy and grace, can give us the desire to share His love with others.

Pray for God to open your heart to sharing the Gospel with everyone you know. Pray for opportunity. Write out your prayer.

EPISODE 36

TAKING THE CHALLENGE

Several months ago we had a 30 day challenge, and we decided we should do it again. Here is a list for you to try for a month. If it looks overwhelming and you are unable to do it every day, then just swap the activity or continue another week. This is not some legalistic ritual, but a way to encourage you to get into a routine. Some activities are personal and others are motivating you to reach out to those around you.

Different activities are scheduled for different days of the week:

- **Sundays** - SCRIPTURE - Read a passage of Scripture
  - examples: verses from this Bible study, from a Sunday morning message, a favorite section, etc.
- **Mondays** - MEMORIZE - Memorize a Scripture verse you can use when sharing with someone
  - examples: about salvation, God's promises, or God's attributes, etc.
- **Tuesdays** - TAKE ACTION - Reach out to others
  - examples: write a note, do a kindness, tell someone about Jesus, etc.
- **Wednesdays** - WORSHIP - Worship God
  - examples: through music, in nature, by giving, etc.
- **Thursdays** - PRAY - Talk to God in prayer

- examples: for the salvation of specific people, for wisdom and discernment, with thankfulness, etc.)

- **Fridays** - FAMILY AND FRIENDS - Connect with family and friends
  - examples: repair a strained relationship, invite a friend to coffee, touch base with a relative, etc.

- **Saturdays** - SERVICE - Service for others
  - examples: take hygiene items to a homeless shelter, mow the lawn of an elderly neighbor, etc.

Try to do some of these things this week. It is amazing how once you intentionally start doing these things, it becomes more routine for you, and you start looking for ways to share the kindness of God with others. Have fun!

EPISODE 37

SERVE HIM WITH ALL YOUR HEART

Our faith is an outpouring from our heart to remain true and serve God with everything within us. There are so many verses about serving God with all your heart. One can only conclude that it is so very important. Have you ever been asked to serve in some way that you feel is not your thing, not your "gift"? I have. Many times. I may not roll my eyes, but I know my attitude is not always the best. It is wonderful to utilize those gifts God has given you, BUT sometimes things just need to happen, stuff just needs to be done. If there is a need, we should have an open heart to meet that need, even if it is not our favorite thing to do.

> *"Only be very careful to follow the commandment and the Law which Moses the servant of the LORD commanded you, to love the LORD your God and walk in all His ways, and keep His commandments and cling to Him, and serve Him with all your heart and with all your soul." Joshua 22:5.*

This is a great verse. It is a command to serve and to do it with all our heart.

QUESTIONS

1. **Look up 1 Samuel 12:24 and Acts 11:23. There is a common thread with these two verses. Both verses say, "See what God has done for you and how amazing He is?! What are you going to do about it? How are you going to worship Him?"**

   What does each verse say that God has done for you or given you? In each verse, what is the action that comes as the result of knowing what God has done?

   ____

   ____

   ____

   ____

   ____

2. **Chapter 2 of Philippians has great instructions for us. Verses 12-15 tell us,**

   > *"So then, my beloved, just as you have always obeyed, not as in my presence only but now much more in my absence, work out your own salvation with fear and trembling, for it is God who is at work in you, both to desire and to work for HIS good pleasure. Do all things without complaining and arguments, so that you will prove yourselves to be blameless and innocent, children of God above reproach in the midst of a crooked and perverse generation, among whom you appear as lights in the world."*

Think about this: when writing this entire letter, Paul is in prison yet he is not complaining, and he tells the people in Philippi not to complain or argue about things. The book of Philippians is al-

ways referred to as the book of Joy, because Paul expresses joy knowing of their faith and he encourages them, and us, to have an attitude of joy.

What are the things that cause you to complain or argue?

How can you work on your attitude in those instances?

____

____

____

____

____

____

Pray about your attitude and ask God to help you be joyful instead, since He is the one working through you.

3. ***God does not always remove our difficult circumstances, but He is able to see us through the tough times in life. Think about something in your life that is difficult right now.***

   Have you seen God work in your life or in the lives of others during this difficult time? Do you see a way that God can use you through it? How can you be a "light in the world"?

____

____

____

____

____

4. ***Here are three very important aspects of our life to think about.***

   i. We need a sincere and genuine faith. God lives in us if we have accepted Christ as our savior.

ii. We need boldness to share our faith with others—not be ashamed of our faith.

iii. We need to be at peace with suffering for the gospel.

What steps can you take to give you the sincere faith of Paul?

5. *How can you serve God with ALL your heart?*

EPISODE 38

LIFT YOUR FEET

Years ago I was in a rafting accident. I was thrown out of the raft going through some rough rapids. Having grown up on a farm with riverfront property, I knew that after the rapids there would be a calm spot, and I would be able to swim to shore. I lifted my feet up, faced forward, and went down the rapids on my back. I did get a few scrapes but sure enough, soon there was a smooth and quiet spot in the river. My sister and the other two people in the raft caught up to me and pulled me into the raft.

We have rapids in our life: times of adversity, hardship and heartache. They have the ability to pull us under and knock us unconscious. What do we do during those times of difficulty? Do we lift our feet? Do we let the water overpower us or do we let the all powerful God help us?

QUESTIONS

1. **When the river of life gets rough, and you get knocked out of your raft, do you fight against the rushing water and get hurt worse? Or are you prepared, and think about the wisest choice, and what you need to do to make it through those rough waters?**

   Read Isaiah 43:2 and Deuteronomy 31:8.

   What happens when we trust God during difficult times?

2. **God is greater than our fears during trials. We are not promised that life will be without struggle. Our faith is our anchor when hard times come. Check out the following scriptures. What will God do?**

   Psalm 34:4-5:

   Psalm 73:23

Psalm 73:26: ______________________________________

____

____

____

3. ***The Sermon on the Mount in Matthew 6 gives us great hope. Specifically, verse 34 tells us,***

> *"So do not worry about tomorrow; for tomorrow will worry about itself. Each day has enough trouble of its own."*

I think the fact that the Sermon on the Mount starts by encouraging believers to love their enemies and care for others BEFORE telling us not to worry, almost shows us that worrying should not be on the forefront of our mind.

Sometimes when I have been the most upset, I think of others who are in worse circumstances, and then I seek out my Bible. Not just to look at verses for comfort but just to read God's Word. Then I am learning who God is. As I know Him more, I trust Him more. Read Matthew chapters 5-7 and learn about God and what is important to Him.

What does 1 Chronicles 16:11 say we should do?

____

____

____

4. ***In Romans 5:3, the apostle Paul says we can "celebrate or glory" in our tribulations (afflictions, distress, trials). Such a hard thing to do, but he goes on to explain what tribulation can bring to our lives. Read Romans 5:3-5 and list the results of trusting God through hard times.***

____

____

5. ***Some tools that can help us as we go through difficulties and trials are:***

   - ***Prayer: God is waiting to listen to your heart and provide comfort and guidance.***
   - ***Our Bible: God's Word has all the answers***
   - ***Sound Teaching: It grounds us and gives us direction.***
   - ***Godly friends: They can help pray for you and provide guidance too.***

If we are praying, learning from God's Word, and seeking Godly counsel, when difficult things happen we are not totally destroyed or consumed because we are prepared - we've lifted our feet.

Have you experienced a time when you've known how to handle a situation because you were prepared? How have you made use of the tools listed above to "lift your feet"?

EPISODE 39

A SINCERE FAITH

I must open this lesson with a passage from 2 Timothy 1. This is so vital to us understanding how to be strong in our faith. I hope it ignites something within you.

> *"I thank God, whom I serve with a clear conscience the way my forefathers did, as I constantly remember you in my prayers night and day, longing to see you, even as I recall your tears, so that I may be filled with joy. For I am mindful of the* ***sincere faith within you****, …For God has not given us a spirit of timidity, but of power and love and discipline. Therefore, do not be ashamed of the testimony of our Lord, or of me His prisoner; but join with me in suffering for the gospel according to the power of God, who has saved us and called us with a holy calling, not according to our works, but according to His own purpose and grace which was granted us in Christ Jesus from all eternity…* ***For this reason*** *I also suffer these things, but I am not ashamed; for I know whom I have believed and I am convinced that* ***He is able to guard*** *what I have entrusted to Him until that day."*

This passage, the entire book actually, tugs at one's heart a bit. Written during Paul's second imprisonment, one gets the distinct impression Paul is aware he will soon die. This is the last letter written by Paul, so we hear a sense of urgency and passion. He is in fact sentenced and executed not long after writing it.

QUESTIONS

1. ***Paul calls Timothy his beloved son. Timothy does not have the self-righteousness of the Pharisees, but genuinely followed God with a pure heart. Timothy is continually on Paul's prayer list. Paul is happy to remember his friend Timothy because of his sincere faith and his love for the gospel of Christ and His people.***

   Read 2 Timothy 1:5 and Philippians 2:20-22. Do you have people in your life that you feel so closely knit to, that you know they walk so closely with their Savior, that you just want to hang with them? I do and I always feel refreshed.

   Make a list of these friends and what it is about them that encourages you in your walk.

   ___

   ___

   ___

   ___

   ___

2. ***Paul also talks about Timothy's Godly heritage and how that upbringing had a big influence on him. Timothy and his family are from Lystra. Paul visited there on his first missionary journey (Acts 14:16-20) and then again on his second (Acts 16:1-5). Timothy's grandmother or mother led him to his genuine faith.***

   God uses parents and grandparents to pass on that legacy. How have you seen this in your own life? Maybe it was not a relative, but maybe a neighbor or friend who influenced you spiritually. Share your story.

   ___

   ___

   ___

3. **Paul encourages Timothy to be strong and bold. It may be that Timothy was on the shy side or soft-spoken. Timothy already cared for his flock, but Paul reminded him to also be bold. Paul encourages Timothy to be bold in 25 places in the pastoral epistles.**

   We need to use the gifts God has given us, but sometimes we are hesitant or do not want to share our faith. Maybe we feel that we don't know what to say, or we get anxious. God gives us a sound mind and self-control - there is no need for panic or confusion. God will help us be bold.

   Do you know of someone who stepped out of their comfort zone and was bold in their faith? How did this inspire you?

4. **How do you know your faith is sincere? What evidence do you see in people you know who have sincere faith?**

5. **What is something you could pray about to help you become stronger in your faith and be purposeful to shine for Christ?**

EPISODE 40

DO NOT GROW WEARY OF DOING GOOD

The phrase "lose heart" refers to how in ancient times a woman in labor feels there is no progress. Considering I had very long labors with my kids, I also felt that way. It is often that way in ministry, but we are told to NOT lose heart. I think being in full-time ministry the past several years has helped me to understand this better. I have thought, I want to share the gospel with the world! But how do I do that? I am just an older woman, speaking to women here and there, and hoping a few people buy my books. I am so thankful God has given me this ministry as a way to reach people I would never be able to reach otherwise, but I still get discouraged at times because it is rare for me to see results.

It has made me more aware of those missionary friends I have who have so many needs. No water or power, language issues, travel issues, danger all around them. And also my pastor and the never ending study, counseling, and encouragement he is to everyone. Constantly. Do they get discouraged and weary? I do, but Paul encourages us to continue to do good.

QUESTIONS

1. ***Read Galatians 6:6-10. Paul is instructing those in Galatia to teach others things of God and to not grow tired of the ebb and flow of life. Do not get discouraged if you cannot see a visible impact in another person's life. God is the one who draws. We are His instrument. Be in it for the long haul: have patience, persistence and perseverance. God will give you the strength to continue to help others, even when it takes a long time; for you have no idea the influence you have in other people's lives. God is using you in someone's life. Do not grow weary!***

   Take a look at Philippians 4:13 and Isaiah 40:31. What do they say?

   ____

   ____

   ____

   ____

2. ***God has His own timing for things. God is working even though we don't see it. We are not always there to "catch the fruit" when someone that we have been praying for and witnessing to for years comes to Christ. But it is not about us. Have you ever met with someone for years and saw no progress, and then years later they contact you and tell you they became a believer? Praise God. Then there are others who we never hear about, but do not forget about them. Keep praying for them even if you lose contact. Remain faithful, steadfast, and do not be discouraged.***

   Make a list of a few people you can contact in the next month. Then act on it.

   ____

   ____

   ____

3. ***People are shocked sometimes when a person goes out of their way to help someone. I was doing errands yesterday, and decided to quickly go through a drive-thru. There was a line. Cars were coming from two different parts of the parking lot. The lady in front of me pushed her way ahead instead of using the zipper method of taking turns and letting the other lane go ahead. So I waved on the truck in the other lane to go in front of me. I did not see this as a big issue, and when I got up to the payment window, the cashier told me the man in the truck had paid for me. It was obviously a big deal to him. It is the little things that show kindness. Be an instrument of God's grace. Being generous is a state of the heart.***

   List 5 ways you can show kindness this week.

   1. ____________________

   2. ____________________

   3. ____________________

   4. ____________________

   5. ____________________

4. ***When I think about the phrase "do not grow weary of doing good", I think of so many missionaries I have heard speak or have shared a meal with through the years. Missionaries who were in a country for 20 years and saw only one convert, but stayed because no other missionary would go there. Or a missionary who slept with a gun because his family was in such a scary country, but who stayed for years because God wanted them there. Or a missionary waiting outside a building every day for months until they finally were given permission to hold a Bible study.***

   Then I look at my obstacles to serving, and they seem very small. The disciples did not even understand what Jesus was

talking about most of the time; many did not understand until after the resurrection. Am I blinded in any way? Do I understand what He has for me to accomplish for His kingdom? I can go 3 months without selling a book or getting a speaking engagement. Then I ask God, "Do You still want me to do this?" I am not kidding when I tell you, the very next day I get a message from a reader thanking me for one of my books that encouraged them in some way. Then I shake my head and scold myself for doubting Him. All in HIS time. He wants us to hang tight, and keep going.

Read Isaiah 41:10 and Matthew 16:24. How can we keep going and serve God?

EPISODE 41

HOPE OF HEAVEN

How do we keep the hope of Heaven in the forefront of our mind? I had a friend in college who once told me to make a sign that said, "Does it count for eternity?" I can't remember what I had done, but I think he thought I had been frivolous; that my actions were not lasting, and not necessary. He said it to me because he thought I needed to hear it. I am now 65 years old. That was long ago but his words are still in my head. "Does it count for eternity?" Is what I am doing making a difference in light of eternity? That does not mean we can't sew a grandchild a dress or decorate a room or have lunch with a friend. BUT I think it really means that we should keep our eyes and mind on the hope God has given us of our eternity with Him. And be thinking of the eternity of those around us.

God promises us eternity if we know Him. Romans 8:18 tells us,

> *"For I consider that the sufferings of this present time are not worthy to be compared with the glory that is to be revealed to us."*

And I can't even fathom how amazing that is for us. But I know for certain it will be incredible. But it is true that while still on this earth we will have trials. Let's take a look at the hope He gives us.

QUESTIONS

1. **2 Corinthians chapter 4 has always been a favorite of mine. Please read the entire chapter. For this question we're focusing on verses 7-12. Paul and his fellow workers in Christ had been going through many hardships. Remember this all followed on the heels of hundreds of Christians being persecuted and killed. Even in our darkest times God is there with us. God is what keeps us going through trials.**

   What do these verses tell us is the result of trials and suffering? What will God do when we go through tough times?

   1 Peter 5:10:________________________________

   ____

   ____

   Romans 5:3-5:________________________________

   ____

   ____

   James 1:2-4: ________________________________

   ____

   ____

2. **Now let's take a look at verses 16-18 of 2 Corinthians chapter 4:**

   "Therefore we do not lose heart, but though our outer person is decaying, yet our inner person is being renewed day by day. For our momentary, light affliction is producing for us an eternal weight of glory far beyond all comparison, while we look not at the things which are seen, for the

things which are seen are temporal, but the things which are not seen are eternal."

This is what my friend from college was referring to.

So how do we incorporate this into our lives so we can help others? What are you doing or what can you do that "counts for eternity"? List three ways.

____

____

____

____

3. ***The older I get the more I think of those in my life who do not know Christ. Thinking about Heaven is one thing. Thinking of Hell is another. I have always prayed for them to accept Christ but not with the urgency I feel now. I wake up at night and pray for them. I think one way I have become more aware is by studying the Word more. As I study the Old Testament, I see God as Holy and Righteous and a Judge. I also see sin and how God hates sin. Then I read the New Testament and see His grace and what happens if you do not accept it.***

   Please read the following verses: Luke 16:19-23; John 5:25-29; Psalm 94:1-2; and Matthew 13:47-50. What do they tell us about what comes after this life, and about judgment?

   ____

   ____

   ____

   ____

4. ***1 Timothy 1:15-16 tells us the good news: God loves us and sent His precious Son (John 3:16). Jesus has taken our place and paid the price for our sins by dying on the cross. And he rose from the dead so we, who believe in Him, might have eternal life. In John 14:1-6, Jesus tells the disciples what he is going to do.***

Share in 2-5 sentences why you believe you will go to Heaven. Keep it short so you could share with someone else.

EPISODE 42

YOU'VE GOT WHAT IT TAKES

Do you sometimes feel unworthy and unable to serve God? Have you felt unprepared and unqualified to tell someone about the salvation Jesus offers? Do you have doubts about being able to minister to others? I do. I have struggled for years to feel worthy of ministry, but I know that He does not want me defeated. He wants me victorious; humble but not doubting. God knows that I am flawed, but He still wants to use me anyway.

You are a child of the one true king. The more we get to know God, the easier it is to share our faith and serve our mighty God. God is faithful. We are not lacking, because He gives gifts to all of us. We have what it takes to serve Him. No matter what flaws or insecurities we have, or how many times we stick our foot in our mouths, He is going to use us.

I pray that God will show you how He wants to use you. Whether you are a new believer or a seasoned believer, you've got what it takes to serve the Lord.

QUESTIONS

1. ***Read 1 Corinthians 1:4-9. This passage was written to people at the church at Corinth. Paul called them saints - people set apart for God from the world. He is very thankful for the church there. Corinth was a very worldly city, but Paul spent a year and a half there, longer than any other city on his journey. He stayed with Priscilla and Aquila, and worked in their tent-making business. There was a caste system in that society with 8 different levels. The people in Corinth did not believe everyone was equal within society, or even within the church. The believers there had many struggles. God granted them grace. He gave them gifts to use.***

   What does this passage say to you?

   ____

   ____

   ____

   ____

   ____

   Paul wanted them to know God would take care of their weaknesses, and God would confirm them to the end, weaknesses and all. God will do the same for you.

2. ***Read these verses about the gifts God gives to believers: I Corinthians 12:4-11 and 12:27-31; Romans 12:6-8; Ephesians 4:11-13; and I Peter 4:9-11.***

   List some ways you believe God has gifted you to be able to serve Him.

   ____

   ____

   ____

   ____

3. ***Did you know that the word "serve" appears 309 times in the Bible? Take a look at the following verses. What do they tell you about "service" to God?***

   1 Samuel 12:24: ______________________________

   ____

   ____

   Romans 12:1: ______________________________

   ____

   ____

   1 Timothy 1:12: ______________________________

   ____

   ____

4. ***We serve a mighty God. He is able to work through us no matter what we do or how we mess up. He'll help us because He loves us so much. He gives us strength to serve Him.***

   How are you serving God? What would you like to start doing? Write down some ways you can use the gifts God has given you to serve others, and to tell them about God's love for them.

   ____

   ____

   ____

   ____

   ____

EPISODE 43

PLANT THE SEED

Dwight L. Moody said, "So *if we only lead one soul to Christ we may set a stream in motion that will flow on when we are dead and gone.*" That is thought provoking, isn't it? I believe we do not really think that we can make a difference, or maybe that we are just a small fish in a huge pond. But there are ripple effects in that pond that go on for generations. By telling someone about our relationship with God through Jesus, we can plant the seed of interest in spiritual things, the seed of knowledge and truth about Jesus and what He has done for us, the seed of salvation. We may not know the impact or outcome of that conversation for years, or ever, but that's ok. We have no idea what someone may accomplish after they accept Christ. They could become a missionary, lead 100 people to Christ, or impact thousands of people. The possibilities are endless...all because you shared your faith with that one person.

QUESTIONS

1. ***Billy Graham was a great example of someone who had a deep desire to share the gospel of Christ with everyone he knew. You may not feel you could shout the gospel to 200,000 people in an enormous venue but you don't need to. YOU need to do what is right for you.***

   God has given us many scriptures telling us to share the gospel. How will you do this? List 3 ways you find easiest to share your faith. Share an example.

2. ***Read Romans 1:16. Do you think this passage applies to you? Being ashamed could just mean being hesitant, reluctant, insecure, etc. Why is it so hard for us to be BOLD?***

3. ***Read 2 Corinthians 3:12-13. What is our "hope"? How do these verses encourage you to "plant the seed"?***

4. ***Many times it is HOW we live our lives, rather than just what we say, that "speaks" to others. Of course, we need to tell people about Jesus, and what He has done so that we can have a relationship with God. How will they know otherwise? But if our conduct does not line up with our words, then our words lose their power.***

   Have you ever had the experience of having your life, and the way you live it, be the major factor in showing someone the path to salvation? Or maybe you saw how a friend or relative lived their Christian life and that drew you to seek the Lord. Write down your experience.

EPISODE 44

THE LORD WILL INSTRUCT YOU

I keep thinking of all the times I failed to listen when God instructed me. This episode is the 44th out of 45 videos on how to live our faith. We have talked about writing your testimony, memorizing verses, serving others, and reaching out to those struggling or in need. We have studied many Bible passages on how to put it all into practice: what God has instructed us to do if we know Him. THAT has been the goal of this series - for you to be purposeful and to Boldly live for God, not ever wavering. And the more we practice these things, the more it becomes a habit and becomes easier for us to share the Gospel with others.

The more we stay in the Word, pray, and fellowship with believers, the more we will want to do these things (or the more we will feel inspired to do them). My prayer for you would be that you become passionate for Christ, that you feel that sense of urgency to share with others God's love, and how they can have a relationship with Him.

QUESTIONS

1. **God wanted Moses to lead the Israelites. Moses told God every excuse he could think of to NOT be the leader. He finally said, "I can't even talk right!" Exodus 4:11-13 tells us God's answer to Moses' excuses:**

   "But the Lord said to him, 'Who has made the human mouth? Or who makes anyone unable to speak or deaf, or able to see or blind? Is it not I the LORD? Now then go, and I Myself will be with your mouth, and instruct you in what you are to say."

   God did not let Moses fail. He is the all powerful God. He will give you the ability you need if you are willing to serve.

   Has there been a time when you shared with someone and God gave you the words to say? Explain.

   ____

   ____

   ____

   ____

   ____

2. **Like Moses, I can doubt that God actually wants to use me. Me who has weaknesses. Me who has fears. Look up the following verses. What do these verses have in common? What do they tell you?**

   Psalm 56:3-4: ______________________________

   ____

   ____

Ephesians 6:10: ______________________________

____

____

Romans 8:26: ______________________________

____

____

Philippians 1:28: ______________________________

____

____

3. **God instructs us to serve Him. 1 Peter 4:10 and Romans 12:11 tell us,**

   "As each one has received a special gift, employ it in serving one another as good stewards of the manifold grace of God".

   "Not lagging behind in diligence, fervent in spirit, serving the Lord."

The definition of "instruct" is: 1) to direct or command someone to do something, especially as an official order. 2) to teach a subject or skill.

So basically we are commanded to serve. It is true we have different gifts and skills God has given us, but we are not to be complacent or fearful.

Share what you believe to be your greatest obstacle to serving God.

____

____

Pray that the Lord would help you overcome this obstacle. We need to step up to our calling. We need to do what God wants us to do: share our faith with others and serve others. He will help us.

EPISODE 45

YOU ARE CALLED

The purpose in doing this video series was to encourage you to intentionally share your faith with others, and to encourage others in their walk of faith. We began the videos during the Covid epidemic. It was such a good time to learn and study. Then, it was recommended to me to make study guides to go with the videos so people could think more about each lesson, and put into practice some of what we were learning.

My prayer for you is that you would be steadfast in serving the Lord. Don't waver in what you "think" you can do, but be courageous like Joshua. We live each day with opportunities. Do we take advantage of them? Do we shove them aside, grieving the Holy Spirit who prods us? I have done that more times than I can count. I can be driving along and someone comes to mind who needs an encouragement note. A month later I realized I never wrote it. But even then I can write a short note - it's never too late.

Maybe, just maybe, these videos and workbooks have helped to embolden you towards the calling God has for you. For He has called you. And He has called me. To serve Him and share the Good News of Jesus with others, so they too can have a relationship with God, and life abundant.

QUESTIONS

1. **Live with purpose. Have confidence in the power God grants us when serving Him. One of the theme verses for our Live Boldly Ministry is Romans 1:16. We shared this verse in a previous chapter, but it is so relevant to our book. Matter of fact, it is on the back of our t-shirts. It reads,**

    "For I am not ashamed of the gospel, for it is the power of God for salvation to everyone who believes, to the Jew first and also to the Greek."

    We can speak with assurance about God and what we believe, and the salvation that is provided through Christ dying for us. These things are to be shared with everyone: Jewish and non-Jewish. That includes everyone.

    List at least five people you have been praying for or want to be praying for to accept Christ.

    ____

    ____

    ____

    ____

    ____

    By writing these names down, it solidifies your intention to pray. Pray for opportunities to reach out to each of these people. If they do not live close by, send them a note or give them a call. Pray for wisdom.

2. **Read 2 Timothy chapter 2. Paul is telling Timothy, and us, to be strong. Remember, Paul is in prison when he is writing this book. Verses 10-13 tell us,**

    "For this reason I endure all things for the sake of those

who are chosen, so that they also may obtain the salvation which is in Christ Jesus and with it eternal glory. It is a trustworthy statement: For if we died with Him, we will also live with Him; If we endure, we will also reign with Him; If we deny Him, He will also deny us; If we are faithless, He remains faithful, for He cannot deny Himself."

Wow! Paul is instructing Timothy to persevere in the work, to keep telling people about salvation through Jesus. He is encouraged to keep going, and God will grant him strength. Sometimes we need that kind of encouragement . We can persist too, not in our own strength, but in the strength God has given us. We can also instruct others to be strong and serve just as Paul did with Timothy.

Have you ever "endured" so others could hear about salvation? How have you continued on through opposition, discouragement or difficulties?

____

____

____

____

____

____

3. **In Peter's first letter, he encourages us to "always be ready" to tell others about our faith in Jesus and the hope we have because of salvation.**

   Read I Peter 3:15-16. What can we do to "be ready"?

____

____

____

What should our demeanor and conduct be when we tell others about our faith?

4. ***Write out how you came to salvation in Jesus and what God has done in your life, so you can be ready to share with others. Include any verses you feel are important for someone seeking God to hear.***

Seek to know God better - read the Bible and pray. Be purposeful in the things you do everyday. God will use you to impact others for Christ as you serve Him. Live BOLDLY!

PERSONAL NOTES

PERSONAL NOTES

PERSONAL NOTES

PERSONAL NOTES

ABOUT THE AUTHOR

Nicki Corinne White has a passion for studying and teaching God's Word. She has been leading Bible studies and discipling young women for many years . She is involved in her local church with both children's ministry and women's ministry. She has a tender heart for those who are hurting and those who are new to church. Nicki hopes to be an encouragement to those around her: lending a listening ear, kind word or a Biblical reminder. She also opens her home to share and serve others through hospitality on a regular basis, and believes we are all called to do this. Nicki feels blessed to have been able to use her story and personal experience to encourage others and hopes to expand this ministry through her writing.

Nicki Corinne grew up in Snohomish, Washington, with her mom, dad and sister. She was adopted at the age of one with her sister, Lisa, into the Maynard family. Nicki went to college at a small Christian Liberal Arts College in Southern California. She met her husband, Craig, after graduating and was married two years later. They moved to the Central Coast of California, then on to the Bay Area where they had their first three children. Five years later, they moved to Boise, Idaho where their fourth child was born. Nicki has worked several jobs including teaching, merchandising, administrative work, and various artist projects. She enjoys spending time outdoors, painting, writing, and spending time with her four children and eight grandkids.

Nicki Corinne has published three books: "Not Really a Princess", "It's Not About The Pie", and "Bold: Living Intentionally in Today's World". She also has published the first and second volumes of "LIVE BOLDLY WORKBOOK" for video episodes 1-15 and episodes 16-30. She looks forward to sharing this third workbook with you and others to complement the 45 episode video series "LIVE BOLDLY".

CONTACT US

Nicki Corinne White is available for book signings and speaking engagements. To get in touch with her team, please email us or message us through her website.

Email:

nickicorinnewhite@gmail.com

Website:

www.liveboldlyministries.com

Social Media:

Facebook Instagram X YouTube

Find all the videos for this workbook on YouTube @nickicorinnewhite7299 (episodes 31-45)

LIVE BOLDLY MINISTRIES

NICKI CORINNE WHITE